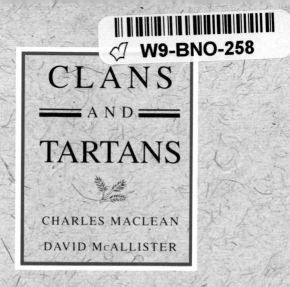

CLANS
AND
TARTANS

CHARLES MACLEAN

DAVID McALLISTER

PELICAN PUBLISHING COMPANY
Gretna 1997

For Jock Stewart, Kildonan, Isle of Arran:
descended from princes and a prince among men

Published by The Appletree Press Ltd., 1995
Published by arrangement in North America by
    Pelican Publishing Company, Inc., 1997

ISBN 1-56554-291-6

Printed in the UAE

Published by Pelican Publishing Company, Inc.
1101 Monroe Street, Gretna, Louisiana 70053

The Origins of Clans and Tartans

Clans

The Gaelic word *clann* simply means "children". It began to be used about a thousand years ago. Prior to this the more ancient and broader word *cenel* described the tribal divisions in the country which became Scotland.

The concept of clanship reaches far into the prehistoric Celtic world. Each community was a little kingdom. Pictland was originally divided into seven and, by the sixth century, the British Kingdoms of Strathclyde in the south-west, Lothian in the south-east, and the Gaelic Kingdom of Dalriada (Argyll) had also emerged.

The social structures and customs which governed these principalities were preserved and developed by the later clan system. Indeed, many chiefs were descended from the ancient kings, according to their genealogists, and, because of the blood-bond which exists between chief and clan, the same can be said of anybody bearing his name. Hence the dignity and pride of the Highlander. "My race is royal" is the motto of Clan Gregor; "I am poor but I am proud. Thank God I am a Maclean" runs a well-known saying.

Modern research suggests that the origins of most clans are more prosaic. Their emergence has much to do with the subordination of the ancient kingdoms to the Scottish Crown during the twelfth and thirteenth centuries, and the opportunities thus created for warlords to "put lands under them" with the assistance of their kindred, and to dominate localities remote from central authority.

The Wars of Independence in the late thirteenth and early fourteenth centuries provided further opportunities, and those clans which supported the triumphant cause of Robert the Bruce were rewarded with grants of land, and the right to dispense justice in the name of the Crown. Conversely, those who opposed him lost territory and status.

The relationship between the clans and the Scottish Crown during the following four centuries was uneasy. The Highland clans spoke a different language, dressed differently, had different customs, different loyalties and were as remote culturally as they were physically from the emerging modern state of Scotland. Their often vaunted independence of central authority was threatening; their loyalty only to their chief and Name was potentially treacherous. Strong kings led expeditions into the Highlands and Islands, hanged chiefs, took hostages against good behaviour, set one clan against another, and generally sought to curb their unruly subjects.

Yet during the Great Civil War of the 1640s and the Jacobite risings of 1689, 1715, 1719 and 1745 most of the clans were royalist. Indeed, it was their support for Prince Charles Edward Stewart's desperate venture to restore his father to the Throne that led directly to the obliteration of the clan system, following the Jacobite defeat at the Battle of Culloden in 1746.

Tartans

There are those who maintain that the kilt is "the garb of Old Gaul" and that the clans have worn individual tartans since time immemorial. Debunkers claim that clan tartans were a nineteenth-century creation, and the kilt was the invention of an Englishman. The truth lies in between.

Checked or striped cloth was worn in Scotland from a remote period. The earliest example of such cloth, a fragment of two colour "dog-tooth" checked woollen fabric – the so-called "Falkirk tartan" – dates from about AD235. But, prior to the sixteenth century, there is no clear evidence of tartan as we would recognize it.

Furthermore, the dress of the Highlandman of the 1500s consisted of a long linen shirt (usually dyed yellow) with a plaid or mantle thrown over it. The legs were bare or covered in long chequered stockings or tight trousers, called *triubhas* (hence "trews"). Only during the sixteenth and seventeenth centuries did the plaid evolve into the *feilidh-mor*, the great kilt (literally "great wrap"), which was the precursor of the *feilidh-beg*, the "little kilt" we wear today.

While there is evidence to support the claim that specific patterns of tartan were worn by individual clans, tartan was not originally an expression of identity. Other emblems, particularly sprigs of plants, worn in the bonnet, served this purpose. The truth is that, in smoke-filled "black houses", the cloth would in all likelihood have been kippered to an indistinguishable hue, and it is certain that plaids were taken as booty on clan raids.

However, there are early references both to identifiable regional colours and patterns, even associated with individual clans. In 1587 Hector Maclean of Duart received a charter for lands in Islay, for which his feu duty was sixty ells of black, white and green cloth. The current Maclean hunting tartan is black, white and green. In a letter to one of his lairds in 1618, Sir Robert Gordon instructed him to "remove the red and white lines from [his tennants] plaides so as to bring their dress into harmony with the other septs" (i.e. branches of the clan). A German woodcut of 1631 shows "Mackay's Highlanders", in the service of the King of Sweden, wearing a uniform pattern of tartan.

In this little book I have selected leading clans, all of them Highland, provided a thumb-nail sketch of their origins and some anecdotes from their histories. Most clans have two or more tartans, for dress and day wear, and some have many (the Stewarts have at least 59 tartans). You can wear what you like, although there is no doubt that wearing "your own" tartan is particularly satisfying.

Tracing Your Ancestors

The Gaels, both Irish and Scots, were passionately keen on their genealogy. Early law forbade that this be written down – it had to be committed to memory, and each important household retained and honoured a *seannachie* to do just this. As a result, any Scot of Highland descent – and often of Lowland families as well – can trace their antecedents back into myth once they connect their line to that of their chief.

For most people, it is ascertaining their more recent ancestors which poses the problem. Several bodies exist in

Scotland to help with this, but before you approach them you should obtain as much information as you can from relatives and family sources, such as family bibles, about names, dates and places of birth, marriage and death.

The modern-day equivalent of the Grand Seannachie of Scotland is Lord Lyon, King of Arms. He has the status of a High Court judge, and his court is at New Register House, West Register Street, Edinburgh EH1 3QN.

The Registrar General for Scotland, also at New Register House, Edinburgh, keeps the records of births, deaths and marriages. These were only recorded centrally after 1855, but Register House also holds most of the Parish Records from 1553–1855.

Roman Catholic Parish Records are held by the Archives of the Roman Catholic Church in Scotland, Columba House, 16 Drummond Street, Edinburgh EH3 6PL.

The Mitchell Library, North Street, Charing Cross, Glasgow G3 7DN holds the International Genealogical Index for Scotland and has copies of the Parish Records on microfiche. It also holds extensive records of Glasgow and West Coast families.

Most towns have considerable local history resources, usually housed in the local library. Tourist Information Centres can guide you to museums, graveyards and clan sites.

The Scottish Genealogical Society, 15 Victoria Terrace, Edinburgh EH1 2JL, the Scots Ancestor Society, 29B Albany Street, Edinburgh EH1 3QN and Scottish Origins, 11a James Court, Lawnmarket, Edinburgh EH1 2NT are available to advise and conduct searches.

Buchanan

Clan Lands:	Loch Lomond (north-east)
Slogan:	*Chlar-innis* (an island in Loch Lomond)
Plant Badges:	Bilberry; Oak

Absalon, son of MacBeth, was granted the lands of *buth chanain* ("the seat/house of the canon" in Old Gaelic, pronounced "Bu-chanan") in 1225 by the Earl of Lennox. They lie to the east of Loch Lomond.

It may be that Absalon himself was "the canon", perhaps a member of one of the ancient Celtic Church families or himself a clergyman. The fortunes of the family were assured by their support for Robert the Bruce during the Wars of Independence, and in the early 1400s Sir Alexander Buchanan distinguished himself when he assisted the French in their efforts to recover territory lost to the English, following the Battle of Agincourt.

Shortly after this, Sir Robert Buchanan married the only daughter of Murdoch Stewart, Duke of Albany and Regent of Scotland. This placed the Buchanans in direct line to the throne. However, the Regent was executed by his cousin, James I, in 1425 and his vast estates confiscated.

It is said that the Buchanan coat of arms, the shield of which is identical to the Royal House of Stewart (except black, rather than red) recollects what might have been.

Cameron

Clan Lands:	Lochaber, Locheil, North Argyll
Slogan:	*Mo righ's, mo dhuthaich*
	("For king and country")
Plant Badges:	Oak; Crowberry

Clan Cameron has been described as "fiercer than fierceness itself" (by no less than General Wolfe, conqueror of Quebec, who faced its members on the field of Culloden) and "the bravest clan among them". Their battle-cry was a promise to feed their enemies' flesh to the dogs: "sons of the hounds, come here and get flesh".

The clan has benefited from a long line of very remarkable chiefs, right down to the present day: the current Lochiel has often been referred to as "The Chief's Chief". Sir Ewen, the 16th Chief (1629–1719), became an implacable royalist after witnessing the brutal execution of Montrose in Edinburgh and held out longer than anyone in Britain against Oliver Cromwell.

His grandson, "The Gentle Lochiel", described as "perhaps the finest highland chief there has ever been", worked hard to improve the lot of his people and brought them out for Charles Edward Stewart in 1745. This was against his better judgement but made the Rising possible, since many other chiefs held back until Lochiel joined the Prince. Over sixty years old, he was badly wounded at Culloden, but escaped to France, where he died in 1748.

After the '45 the Locheil estates were forfeited, but they were restored in the 1780s, and the Cameron chiefs still live in their ancestral homelands.

Campbell

Lands:	Argyll, Cawdor, Loudoun and Breadalbane
Slogan:	*Cruachan* (a mountain in Argyll)
Plant Badges:	Fir Club Moss; Bog Myrtle

At the time of the eclipse of the clan system in the mid-eighteenth century, Clan Campbell was the most powerful clan in Scotland, and the patronage and influence of its many grandees persisted down to modern times. During the nineteenth century there were fifteen noble branches – i.e. headed by a peer.

The first Campbell to appear in Argyll married an heiress in the early 1200s and the name derived from *cam-beul*, "crooked mouth". His son was knighted in about 1280, as Sir Colin Campbell of Lochawe, and by the time he died he was known as *Cailean Mor* – Colin the Great.

The Chiefs of Clan Campbell are known to this day as *Mac Cailean Mor* – the Son of Great Colin. Indeed, there is a charming story of an old Campbell woman who, when she was told that her chief's son was to marry the daughter of Queen Victoria, said: "Her Majesty'll be a proud woman the day, what wi'her dochter gettin' mairrit on the son o' MacCailean Mor".

Sir Colin's immediate descendants supported King Robert Bruce (one of them, Sir Neil, married Bruce's sister) and for three centuries the family advanced themselves by supporting the Crown. The 1st Earl of Argyll was made Lord Chancellor and Master of the Royal Household in 1464 (an office which eventually became hereditary in his family); the 2nd Earl

died on Flodden Field; the 3rd Earl became Warden of the Marches and Lord Justice General of Scotland (which title also became hereditary in the family for a long time) – and so on.

By the time of the 7th Earl (1584–1638), the Campbells were the paramount clan and their chiefs could bid for the highest positions in the land, as of right. Sir Iain Moncreiffe charmingly puts it: "Thenceforward, Campbell rule of the West Coast inched forward remorselessly, using statecraft, legal cunning and moral courage to combine the Parchment with the Sword".

Fraser

Lands:	East Lothian, then Aberdeenshire and north of Loch Ness
Slogan:	*Caisteal Dhuni* ("Castle Downie")
Plant Badge:	Yew

Of French origin, the name first appeared in Scotland around 1160, with one Simon Fraser, who held lands in Keith (East Lothian). A descendant faught with Wallace, and was hanged, drawn and quartered for his patriotism. His cousin and chief was Robert the Bruce's Lord Chamberlain and married the king's sister. His descendants, who became the Frasers of Philorth, now Lords Saltoun, are chief of the whole Name of Fraser.

The Highland Frasers – Clan Fraser of Lovat – trace their ancestry to the Lord Chamberlain's brother, Sir Simon, who married an heiress and acquired lands in the Aird. Their chief has ever since been known as *MacShimi*, "Son of Simon".

Another Simon Fraser, 11th Lord Lovat (known as the "The Old Fox"), was created Duke of Fraser by "The King over the Water" for his support in the '45 Rising, but he was captured and beheaded on Tower Hill in 1747, the last peer so to be executed. His estates were forfeited, but his son was pardoned and raised 1800 Frasers to fight in Canada.

The peerage was restored in 1837, and during the Boer War the 16th Lord Lovat raised the Lovat Scots, the antecedents of the Commandos, and his son, the 22nd *MacShimi*, was a distinguished commando leader during the Second World War.

14

Gordon

Lands:	Aberdeenshire
Slogan:	*An Gordonach!* ("A Gordon!")
Plant Badge:	Ivy

Gordons first appear in Berwickshire during the twelfth century. They may have been of Anglo-Norman descent, or possibly Ancient British. Sir Adam, lord of Gordon, was granted the lordship of Strathbogie, Aberdeenshire, by Robert the Bruce (120 square miles in extent) and renamed the family seat "Huntly", after part of his lands in Berwickshire. In 1436, Sir Alexander was created Lord Gordon, and in 1447 his son was raised to the title Earl of Huntly. By the end of the fifteenth century the Gordons were the principal power in the north-east, their chiefs known as "Cock o' the North" (as they are to this day).

George, 4th Earl of Huntly, became Chancellor of Scotland and Lieutenant-General of the North. Such was his power that he could contemplate establishing a state of near-independence from the Crown for his northern territories. This was his undoing. Shortly after she was crowned, Mary Queen of Scots led an army into Aberdeenshire and defeated Huntly who died of a stroke when he was brought into the Royal presence. His body was embalmed and tried for treason six months later.

In 1599, the 6th Earl was made Marquess of Huntly. The 2nd Marquess led the Royalist faction in Scotland during the Civil War, but his refusal to co-operate with Montrose ultimately led to his defeat. He was executed in 1649. His

son, Lord Louis Gordon, however, became the 1st Duke of Gordon in 1684.

During the '15 and '45 Risings the Gordons backed both sides. The 3rd Duke supported the Hanoverians, while his brother, Lord Louis Gordon raised a regiment for Prince Charles Edward, and went into exile with him in 1746. The dukedom became extinct with the death of the 5th Duke, and the marquessate passed to a kinsman, from whom the present chief descends.

Another branch of the family became Earls of Aberdeen in 1682. The 4th Earl was Prime Minister of Great Britain from 1852–55, and the 7th Earl, who was Governor General of Canada from 1893–98, became Marquess of Aberdeen in 1916.

Grant

Lands:	Strathspey, Glenmoriston, Glenurquhart
Slogan:	"Stand Fast Craigellachie" (a hill in Grant country)
Plant Badge:	Pine

The name is of Norman origin, from *le Grand*, and the family came to Scotland through marriage to a Bisset heiress in the mid-thirteenth century. Their original lands were in Stratherrick, north of Inverness, and by 1258 Sir Laurence le Grant was sheriff of that town.

The clan supported Bruce during the Wars of Independence, and as a result they were granted the lands which they still largely populate, in Strathspey, Glenmoriston and Glenurquhart. Their power in the region was further consolidated by the marriage of Sir John Grant to Maud, heiress of Glencairnie and a scion of the ancient Earls of Strathearn. His lands were made a free barony in 1493. In 1536 his son built a stronghold, called originally Freuchie Castle and later Castle Grant, when the Grants of Freuchie became known simply as Lairds of Grant. This family is the progenitor of the Earls of Seafield, the Grants of Glenmoriston and of Corrimony.

For two centuries the Grants were Royalists, then Sir James Grant, known popularly as "The Highland King" on acount of his power and influence, supported William and

Mary in the late seventeenth century, and as a result the barony of Freuchie was made a Regality, in effect a semi-independent state, in which the chief had power not only to punish wrongdoers but to regulate commercial matters such as weights and measures. This status was removed in 1747, with the abolition of hereditable jurisdictions.

The last time the fiery cross was sent round the Highlands was in 1820, to muster Clan Grant in support of their chief, whose brother was standing as M.P. for Elgin, and who had been barricaded into his town house by supporters of the other candidate. Eight hundred clansmen turned up and "the townspeople fled at their coming".

Lamont

Lands:	Cowal
Motto:	Ne Parcas Nec Spernas
	(Neither spare nor dispose)
Plant Badge:	Crab Apple

Clan Lamont descends from Ladman who was Lord of Cowal (south Argyll) in 1238, and whose descent was from the O'Neil Kings of Ulster. John Lamont of Inveryne was knighted in 1539 and had his principal seat at Toward Castle, where he entertained Mary, Queen of Scots, in 1563.

In the following century the Lamonts were Royalists, which brought them into conflict with their mighty and rapacious neighbours, the Campbells, whose chief, the Marquess of Argyll, was the leader of the Covenanting party.

In 1646 the latter invaded the Lamont lands and forced their chief to surrender his castles of Toward and Ascog, upon promise of safe conduct for his family and clansfolk. No sooner had they agreed than the Campbells siezed Sir James and about two hundred of his clan. They held the chief at Dunstaffnage Castle for five years (without allowing him to change his clothes); the other prisoners they took to the kirkyard at Dunnoon and there "they most cruelly murthered, without assyse or lorder of law, by shotts, by durks, by cutting their throats, as they doe with beasts, above ane hundred, and lastly they hanged on one tree thirty and six at one time of the chiefs and speciall gentlemen of that name,

and before they were half hanged they cutt them down and threw them in by dozens in pitts prepared for the same; and many of them striveing to ryse upon their feet were violently holden down untill that by throwing earth in great quantity upon them they were stifled to death".

In 1661, when the Marquess of Argyll was brought to trial following the Restoration of King Charles II, the massacre of the Lamonts was one of the charges which led to his execution.

The Lamonts of Lamont continued to live in Cowal until the last of their old lands were sold by the 21st Chief in 1893. The present chief lives in Australia.

Macdonald

Lands: The Southern Isles, South Argyll
Slogan: *Fraoch Eilean* (an island in Argyllshire)
Plant Badge: Heather

At the height of their power, the Macdonald Lords of the Isles ruled most of the West Highlands and much of the Northern Highlands as absolutely as kings. Indeed, the ancestors of this, the greatest of the clans, even styled themselves "King of the Isles".

Their progenitor was Somerled, a great warrior who held the Southern Isles and the mainland from Kintyre to Ardnamurchan as a vassal of the King of Norway and who died fighting the King of Scots in 1164. His realm was divided between his descendants, one of whom (his grandson Donald) was name-fether of the Macdonalds.

Through inheritance and marriage the Macdonald chiefs gradually reunited and even expanded Somerled's kingdom. By the early fifteenth century, as Lords of the Isles and Earls of Ross, they were once again independent princes, holding their own parliaments and making treaties with the Kings of England.

The kings of Scots were naturally jealous of such power and in 1493 James IV led a successful expedition into the Isles to crush the Lordship. Although attempts were made over the following half century to ressurect it, the empire of the Isles remained divided between nine more or less

independent branches, including the Macdonalds of Clanranald (who played a key role in the '45 Rising), Glengarry, Ardnamurchan, Glencoe, Keppoch (who styled themselves MacDonnell) and Sleat.

The chiefs of the latter branch were recognised as Macdonald of Macdonald in 1680 and were raised to the peerage in 1776. The present Lord Macdonald still lives at Sleat, in the Isle of Skye.

Gaelic culture was at its height during the Lordship, patronised and nurtured by Macdonald chiefs. It is no wonder that later bards sang mournfully that "It is no joy without Clan Donald. It is no strength to be without them."

Macdougall

Lands:	Lorne (mid Argyll)
Slogan:	*Buaidh no bàs* ("Victory or Death")
Plant Badge:	Bell heather; Cypress

Dougall was the son of Somerled, King of the Isles (see Macdonald), who inherited the central portion of his father's realm, including Lorne on the mainland and the southern Hebrides apart from Islay. His great-grandson lost most of this territory following the accession of Robert the Bruce, since he had supported the other side.

Ewen Macdougall, Lord of Lorne, married a grand-daughter of Robert the Bruce, and part of the mainland territories were restored to the family, but he had no male heir, so the lands and title passed with his daughter to the Stewarts (later the Stewarts of Appin).

The male line and chiefship was continued by the Macdougalls of Dunollie. For a brief period in 1686 it looked as if their ancient title to all Lorne would be restored, following the forfeiture and execution of the Campbell Earl of Argyll (and Lord Lorne), but the next chief was himself forfeited for supporting the Jacobite cause in the 1715 rising.

The chiefs of Macdougall still live close to the ruins of Dunollie Castle, where their ancestors have lived since time immemorial.

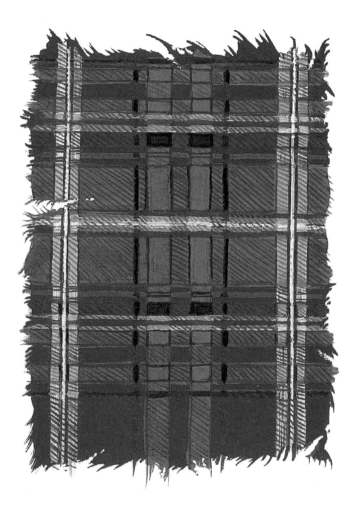

Macgregor

Lands:	Glenstrae, Glenorchy, Glenlochy, Glenlyon, Glengyle
Slogan:	*'S rioghal mo dhream* ("Royal is my race")
Plant Badge:	Pine

Tradition maintains that Gregor was the son of King Kenneth Macalpin in the eighth century – hence the clan's motto – but the first certain chief of Clan Gregor was Gregor "of the Golden Bridles" in the fourteenth century. The clan's heartland was perilously close to that of the powerful Clan Campbell, and the Macgregors suffered mightily for this geographical fact.

In 1519 the Campbells managed to establish their own nominee as Chief of Clan Gregor and laid legal claims to part of the Macgregor lands. The Macgregor chiefs were forced to wage a guerilla war in the mountains of Argyll and Perthshire, and their clan became known as "The Children of the Mist".

In 1603 James VI issued an Order in Council outlawing the entire clan and even forbidding the name Macgregor, on pain of death. The chief, Alexander Macgregor of Glenstrae, was hanged with eleven of his gentlemen in Edinburgh the following year and the clan was scattered and harried, even hunted out with bloodhounds. Of the chief's immediate

family during the following century, twenty-two members were hanged, four beheaded, three murdered (two by arrows in the back) and five died in battle. Many Macgregors adopted other names.

The penal laws against Clan Gregor were not repealed until 1774, and shortly afterwards 826 members of the clan petitioned that General John Murray of Lanrick, the direct descendant of the rightful Macgregor chiefs, be recognised as chief. He was made a baronet in 1795 and his descendants are still Chiefs of the Children of the Mist.

Macinnes

Lands:	Morvern
Motto:	*Ghibht dhe Agus an Righ*
	("By the Grace of God and King")
Plant Badge:	Holly

"Innes" is from *Aonghais* – Angus – who may have been the son of Erc, King of Dalriada (Northern Ireland) in the fifth century, who arrived with his two brothers and 150 warriors to carve out the Kingdom of Dalriada for themselves in Argyll. If this is true, Clan Macinnes, as part of the *Cenel Aonghais* – "the kindred of Angus" – will have originated in Islay.

In historical times the family first appears in Morvern – indeed, is described as "one of the principal names" in that part by the twelfth century – and was still in possession of Kinlochaline Castle in 1645. Shortly after this it would appear that the clan fragmented and lost its chief, for the *Clan Aonghais* came to acknowledge Campbell of Craignish as their chief, and accordingly fought for the Hanoverian side during the Jacobite Risings.

Another branch became hereditary archers to the Mackinnon chiefs in Skye. This is alluded to in the family crest, which is an arm holding a bow.

Mackay

Lands:	Strathnaver, Caithness
Slogan:	*Bratach Bhan Chlann Aoidh* ("The White Banner of Clan Mackay")
Plant Badge:	Great Bullrush

In Gaelic the name is *Mac-Aoidh* (*Aoidh* or *Aedh* being a form of "Hugh") but who this Hugh was is uncertain. Some authorities maintain he was the 1st Earl of Fife, elder brother of Alexander I (1107–24), and David I (1124–1153) who was debarred from the throne because he was also Abbot of Dunkeld, whose descent was from the ancient "Kings" of Moray. His son, Malcolm Macaedh, married a sister of Somerled, King of the Isles, and became Earl of Ross (1156). His son-in-law became Earl of Caithness, Lord of Strathnaver, where, by the fourteenth century, the clan had become established.

By the fifteenth century the chief of Mackay could raise 4000 men from Strathnaver, a position of such strength that he was able to marry the sister of the Lord of the Isles. However, during the following 500 years the Mackay lands were pressed, and ultimately annexed and cleared, by the Earls of Sutherland.

In 1626 Sir Donald Mackay raised a force of 3000 men to fight in Europe for the Elector Palatine, Charles I's brother-in-law. Sir Donald was raised to the peerage as Lord

Reay in 1628, and later fought for Gustavus Adolphus, King of Sweden and champion of the Protestant cause.

The second Lord Reay's father-in-law was the General Mackay who commanded the Williamite army at Killiecrankie (1689) and his son became a general in the Dutch service and raised the famous Mackay's Scotch Regiment. This branch of the family were eventually raised to the Dutch baronage as Baron Ophemert in 1822.

The Sutherlands managed to acquire the Mackay country of Strathnaver in 1875, and Ophemert became the 10th Lord Reay.

Mackenzie

Lands:	Ross and Cromarty, Lewis
Slogan:	*Tulach Ard* (a mountain in Kintail where the clan rallied)
Plant Badge:	Holly; Deer Grass

Clan MacCoinnich, the Mackenzies, once controlled huge territories in northern Scotland, with lands stretching from the North Sea to the Minch, including the island of Lewis.

By 1267 the family had lands in Kintail and a castle at Eilean Donan, and by the fifteenth century their chief could raise 2000 warriors. In 1427 Alexander, 7th Chief of Kintail, was one of the chiefs summoned to a parliament at Perth by King James I, at which the Lord of the Isles was imprisoned. Mackenzie became a royalist and his ancestors remained so, benefiting mightily from their support for the Stuart cause and then losing almost everything.

Following the downfall of the Macdonalds, who were Earls of Ross as well as being Lords of the Isles, a grateful king James III granted the Mackenzie chief extensive forfeited lands in Ross-shire. Kintail was made a free barony in 1508. John Mackenzie fought for James IV at Flodden (1513) and was one of the few Scottish nobles to survive. He fought the English at Pinkie (1547), and his grandson supported Mary Queen of Scots at the Battle of Langside (1568). By 1609, when Kenneth, 12th Chief, became 1st Lord of Kintail, the clan lands extended from the Black Isle to Gairloch, and soon after this date they took the Isle of Lewis from the Macleods.

The 2nd Lord Mackenzie was created Earl of Seaforth by James VI and was Charles II's Secretary of State in Scotland. The 4th Earl was made a Knight of the Thistle by James VII, and later a marquis in the Jacobite peerage. He fought for King James at the Battle of the Boyne and went into exile with his king. His son, the 5th Earl, joined the Earl of Mar in 1715, fought at Sheriffmuir and also went into exile in France. He was attainted and his estates forfeited, but his grandson was able to buy back the old Mackenzie lands and was restored to the Earldom of Seaforth in 1771.

The male line of the Seaforths died out in 1815, as prophesied by – and following the curse of – the Brahan Seer.

Mackinnon

Lands:	Mull, then Skye
Slogan:	*Cuimhnich Bas Ailpein*
	("Remember the Death of Alpin")
Plant Badges:	St Columba's Flower; Scots Pine

The battle-cry of the Mackinnons associates the clan with the King of the Dalriadic Scots who was killed by King Brude of the Picts in 837, and with the king who finally united the two kingdoms, Kenneth MacAlpin. The Mackinnons are "The Sons of Fingon", a high-born prelate in the thirteenth century, of the noble kindred of St Columba. Several generations of their chiefs were Abbots of Iona, representing the traditions of the ancient Celtic Church (which, among other differences, allowed its clergy to marry) against those of Rome and the Benedictine Order. Mackinnon's Cross on Iona was erected in 1489 by the father of the last abbot. The latter's elaborate tomb is in Iona Cathedral.

By 1400 the Mackinnons had lost most of their territory in Mull to the Macleans, and their power base shifted to Skye, where they had been granted lands in by King Robert Bruce.

Throughout the seventeenth centuries the Mackinnons were ardent Royalists. In 1618 Charles I elevated the estate of their chief into a barony. During the 1640s the Mackinnons fought under Montrose, and in 1651 Sir Lachlan Mackinnon saved King Charles II's life on the battlefield of Worcester, for which service he was there and then created knight banneret, the only time such an honour has been bestowed

on the field of battle. After the battle, however, the kilted
Highlanders were an obvious target for the King's enemies,
and it is said that some 200 were killed on their way home.

Sir Lachlan's son brought 150 Mackinnons out during
the '15 Rising and, after defeat at Sheriffmuir, was forfeited.
This did not deter him from bringing his clan out again in
1745, and after Culloden, when Bonnie Prince Charlie was
on the run, he sheltered the Prince in Skye. For this he was
incarcerated on a prison ship for a year, then tried for high
treason. He was over 70, and this fact, combined with his
dignity at his trial secured his aquittal. In 1790 the Mackinnon
lands had to be sold for debt; the chief's direct line died out
with the next generation and many of the clan emigrated.

Mackintosh

Clan Lands:	Badenoch and Lochaber
Slogan:	Clan Chattan
Plant Badge:	Red Whortleberry

Mackintosh is *Mac-an-Toiseach*, "Son of the Leader" or "Captain". The people led by the Mackintosh chiefs were the *Clan Chattan* ("The Clan of the Cats"), a powerful confederation of families which included the Macphersons, Macgillivrays, Davidsons, Macbeans, Macleans of Dochgarroch and (later) Farquharsons.

Mackintosh tradition holds that clan ancestors were the ancient Macduff Earls of Fife, one of whom, Angus, married the heiress to the Captaincy of *Clan Chattan* in 1291. They supported Robert the Bruce during the Wars of Independence and continued to feud against Bruce's rivals, the Comyns, for two centuries. One authority maintains that the famous Trial by Combat fought between two clans in the presence of King Robert III and his court in 1396 was between Mackintosh and Comyn.

The seat of The Mackintosh is at Moy, south of Inverness. Here, in 1746, Lady Anne Mackintosh received Bonnie Prince Charlie. An attempt to capture him there was made by 1500 government troops, but they were deceived into thinking they had blundered into the midst of the Jacobite army by 5 of Lady Anne's retainers and fled. The incident is known to history as "The Rout of Moy". The clan suffered heavily on the battlefield of Culloden, where there is a stone commemorating the *Clan Chattan* dead.

Maclachlan

Lands:	South Argyll
Motto:	*Fortis et Fidus* ("Brave and Trusty")
Plant Badge:	Mountain Ash

Tradition maintains that the Maclachlans descend from the Kings of Ulster, who were driven out by King Brian O'Neill in 1241. The clan takes its name from Lachlan *Mor*, a powerful chief on Loch Fyne in the thirteenth century, after whom are also named Strathlachlan, Lachlan Bay, and Castle Lachlan, where the present Maclachlan of Maclachlan still lives.

The Maclachlans were consistent Jacobites. They formed part of Viscount Dundee's victorious army at Killicrankie in 1689, and of the Earl of Mar's less successful army at Sheriffmuir in 1715. In 1745 they rallied to Prince Charles Edward's standard, joining him at Prestonpans. Lachlan Maclachlan of Maclachlan received a colonel's commission and was made Commissary General of the Jacobite army. He was killed by a cannonball while he was leading 300 Maclachlans and Macleans at Culloden.

Thereafter a government ship came up Loch Fyne and bombarded Castle Lachlan. The estates were declared forfeit for treason, but since the chief had sensibly transferred them to his son over a decade before, the family were allowed to remain on their lands and, during the early years of the nineteenth century, they built a new castle not far from their ancient keep.

Maclean

Clan Lands:	Mull, Morvern, Ardgour, Coll, Tiree
Slogan:	*Bas no Beatha* ("Death or Life")
Plant Badges:	Crowberry; Holly

The Macleans are the "Sons of Gillean of the Battle-axe", a thirteenth century war-lord who "put lands under him" in Morvern, but the family made good the following century through the exploits of Lachlan *Lubanach* ("The Wily") and Hector *Reganach* ("The Crafty"). These bold brothers kidnapped the Lord of the Isles and obliged him to grant them wide territories in Mull, the role of Senechal of the Isles (i.e. Steward) and the hand of his daughter in marriage to Lachlan.

Lachlan founded the chiefly houses of Duart (the high chief), Coll and Ardgour; Hector, those of Lochbuie, Dochgarroch and Kingairloch. Alas, there was little love between the two branches. In the sixteenth century Hector "the Great" of Duart had Ian "the Toothless" of Lochbuie imprisoned on the island of Cairnburgh with no company apart from a mis-shapen crone, to prevent him siring an heir. He succeeded nevertheless, and Murdoch "the Stunted" was the result.

So long as the Macdonalds ruled the Isles, the Macleans were their most loyal supporters, but in the vacuum following the collapse of the Lordship at the end of the 1400s the Macleans made their peace with the Crown and set about conquering former Macdonald territories. The feud lasted 100 years, and by the end of it both clans were so utterly

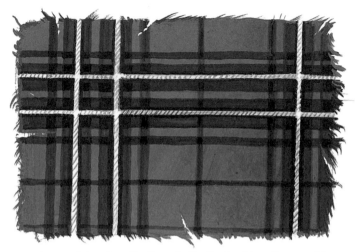

exhausted that the wily Campbells, Earls of Argyll, were able to buy up Duart's debts, and then obtain court orders for the annexation of most of the Maclean lands.

Throughout the Civil War the Macleans vigorously supported the Royalists, and when that cause was lost, the high chiefs went into exile. Sir Hector Maclean of Duart returned to take part in the 1715 and 1745 Risings. On the latter occasion he was captured before the rising began and locked in the Tower of London for its duration. The clan was brought out by Maclean of Drimnin, who died at Culloden.

Subsequent chiefs have all been distinguished soldiers, and the 25th Chief, Sir Fitzroy, managed to buy back Duart Castle in 1911 and restore it.

Macleod

Lands:	Skye, Harris, Lewis, Assynt
Motto:	Hold Fast
Plant Badge:	Juniper

Leod, from whom the clan descend, was the younger son of Olaf the Black, one of the last Norse Kings of Man and the North Isles, who died in 1237. He held lands in Harris and part of Skye and aquired Dunvegan Castle and much of the rest of Skye by marriage to an heiress. Twenty-one generations of Macleod chiefs have lived at Dunvegan ever since.

Leod's sons founded the two great branches of the clan: Siol Torquil, the Macleods of Lewis (until they were overthrown by the Mackenzies in the early seventeenth century), and of Assynt, and Siol Tormod, the Macleods of Dunvegan, Harris, Raasay and Glenelg. The latter branch was acknowledged as chiefs of the whole Name by the sixteenth century.

Two very able chiefs, Alasdair *Crotach* ("Hunch-backed") and Ruaraidh *Mor* ("The Great"), consolidated the clan's power and prestige during the sixteenth century, while other western clans were falling foul of royal authority. The latter was knighted by James VI in 1603 and established Dunvegan as the cultural centre of the isles.

The clan supported Charles I and Charles II during the Civil War, and over 500 Macleods were killed at the Battle

of Worcester in 1651. It took several generations to recover from such losses, and this, combined with resentment against the King's failure to reward the clan after the Restoration, prevented all but the Macleods of Raasay from supporting the Jacobite cause.

After the failure of the '45 Rising and the general collapse of Gaelic society which followed, the Macleods of Dunvegan distinguished themselves by the support they provided for their clanspeople, maintaining doctors and teachers, providing employment and refusing to clear their estates as so many others did.

Macnab

Lands: Glendochart (Strathfillan)
Motto: *Timor Omnis Abesto*
               ("Let fear be far from all")
Plant Badge: Pine; Bramble

The Macnabs are *Clann-an-Aba*, "Children of the Abbot", and the abbot in question was that of Glendochart, a descendant of St Fillan, who was a prince of the Dalriadic royal house of Lorn and who died in 703.

Until the thirteenth century the Abbot of Glendochart still ranked on a par with the Earls of Atholl and Menteith, and when the ancient Celtic abbacies were dissolved the family continued to be prominent. Malcolm de Glendochart signed the Ragman's Roll (1296) and Angus Macnab was brother-in-law to John Comyn, Robert Bruce's opponent as claimant to the Scottish throne – a fact which led to the forfeiture of the Macnab lands, subsequent to Bruce's success. The clan's fortunes were somewhat restored by Gilbert Macnab's confirmation in the Barony of Bovain in Glendochart by David II in 1336.

The Macnab lands were much added to during the fifteenth century, but the family ran into debt and were obliged to mortgage them to Campbell of Glenorchy in 1552. "Smooth John" Macnab brought his clan out for Montrose and was appointed to garrison Kilsyth Castle, where he was captured after a daring breakout and sentenced to death. He escaped on the eve of his execution and led 300 Macnabs to support King Charles on the battlefield of

Worcester (1651), where he was killed.

Connections with the Campbells prevented the Macnab chiefs from participating in the Rising of 1715, and during the '45, the 15th chief, who was a major in the Hanoverian army, was imprisoned by in Doune Castle.

Francis Macnab, 16th chief, was a notable character. Strikingly tall, he made a big impression on London society during a visit in 1800 and was memorably painted by Raeburn. He was, however, the last chief in the direct male line, and shortly after his death his successor had to emigrate to Canada. Archibald Corrie Macnab managed to buy back the old chiefly home at near Killin and his nephew is now the 23rd Macnab of Macnab.

Macneil

Lands:	Barra, Gigha, Colonsay
Slogan:	*Buaidh no bas* ("Victory or death")
Plant Badge:	Seaweed

The Macneils justifiably claim descent from Niall of the Nine Hostages, High King of Ireland during the fourth century and founder of the great O'Neil dynasty, but they take their name from another Niall, who arrived in Barra in about 1050. Neil Macneil, 5th of Barra, was described as a "prince" at a council of the Isles in 1252. His son Neil *Og* (Younger) fought for Robert the Bruce at Bannockburn and was rewarded with a grant of land in Kintyre and the island of Gigha. Gilleonan, 9th of Barra, received a charter from the Lord of the Isles for Barra and Boisdale in 1427.

The 12th chief was officially described as an "hereditary outlaw" and was known as "Ruari the Tartar" and "the last of the Vikings" on account of his piratical raiding. He was imprisoned by his son in 1610, another Neil *Og*, who later led a regiment of cavalry for King Charles I at the Battle of Worcester. His grandson, Ruari *Dubh* ("Black Roderick"), received a royal charter for his lands in Barra as a free barony in 1688, led his clan at Killiecrankie and rallied to the Jacobite standard during the '15 Rising.

These Jacobite sympathies led to Roderick's son being consigned to a prison ship during the '45 Rising, although his estates were not forfeited. The 21st chief, General Roderick Macneil was obliged to sell Barra in 1838 and the chiefship passed to a cousin in America. The father of the present chief was able to buy back and restore the castle of his ancestors.

Macpherson

Lands:	Badenoch
Slogan:	*Creag Dubh Chloinn Chatain*
	("The Black Rock of *Clan Chattan*")
Plant Badge:	Boxwood; White Heather

The Macphersons are "the sons of the parson", a reference to the old Celtic Church which allowed its clergy to marry. The eponymous parson is believed to be *Mhuireach* (or Murdo) *Catanach*, a priest in Kingussie, Badenoch. The clan formed part of the Clan Chattan Confederation (see Mackintosh), and disputed the chiefship of Clan Chattan with the Mackintoshes for many centuries.

Tradition has it that King Robert Bruce granted the lands in Badenoch to the chief of the Macphersons, on condition that he wage war against the Comyns in that district. This chief had three sons, Kenneth, Iain and Gillies, and the Macphersons are sometimes known as "The Clan of the Three Brothers". Kenneth's decendant, Donald Mor, was the first to use the name "Macpherson".

Ewen Macpherson of Cluny brought his clan out for Prince Charles Edward in 1745 and defeated a numerically superior force at Clifton Moor in Westmorland. After the battle of Culloden, Cluny was hidden by his clanspeople for nine years in a skilfully constructed cave on Ben Alder, known as "Cluny's Cave", despite a reward of £1000 being offered for his capture. He finally escaped to France in 1755.

William Macpherson "the Purser" was killed at Falkirk in 1746, and his nephew was James Macpherson of Balavil, "discoverer" of the poems of Ossian, the Gaelic Homer.

MacRae

Lands: Kintail
Slogan: *Sgur Urain* (A mountain in Kintail)
Plant Badge: Fir Club Moss

In Gaelic the name is rendered Macrath, "Son of Grace", and may indicate ecclesiastical origins. The earliest Macraes were to be found near Inverness, but removed to Kintail in Wester Ross in the fourteenth century, where they became supporters of the powerful Mackenzies of Seaforth (see *Mackenzie*) and Constables of Eilean Donan Castle. They were known as "Mackenzie's shirt of mail"!

Duncan Macrae was given lands at Inverinate following his successful defence of Eilean Donan against the Macdonalds of Sleat in 1539, when he managed to kill the Macdonald chief with an arrow. This branch of the family became the chiefly line and were Chamberlains of Kintail for several generations.

Munro

Lands:	Easter Ross
Slogan:	*Caisteal Folais na theine*
	("Castle Foulis in flames")
Plant Badge:	Common Club Moss

The derivation of the name Munro is obscure – probably a now-lost place-name – but since the twelfth century there have been Munros in Easter Ross, on the north side of the Cromarty Firth. This country is called Ferindonald, "the Land of Donald", and the Munros understand this to have been the name of their first chief. The present chief, Munro of Foulis, still lives in the home of his ancestors, Foulis Castle, from the top of which a signal beacon was lit to gather the clan under arms. Hence the Munro slogan *Caisteal Folais na theine*, ("Castle Foulis in flames").

Robert Munro of Foulis supported Bruce at Bannockburn, and a descendant married a neice of Queen Euphemia, wife of King Robert II (1371–90). The 12th Chief was knighted by James IV (1488–1513).

During the seventeenth and eighteenth centuries the clan produced a number of outstanding soldiers. The 18th Chief, Robert, raised and led a large company of Munros in the Protestant army of King Gustavus Adolphus of Sweden during the Thirty Years War (1618–48). His son was made a baronet by Charles I (1634).

The 6th Baronet of Foulis was the first Commanding Officer of the Black Watch, which he commanded at Fontenoy in 1745. He died valorously the following year at the Battle of Falkirk, fighting against the Jacobites, and was given an honourable funeral, attended by all the Jacobite chiefs.

The following century, General Sir Charles Munro of Foulis, 9th Baronet, commanded a Division of the Columbian revolutionary army under Simon Bolivar. James Munroe of Virginia (1758–1831) was 5th President of the United States and served two terms.

Robertson

Lands:	Atholl
Slogan:	*Garg'n uair dhuis gear*
	("Fierce when roused")
Plant Badge:	Bracken

The Robertsons descend from Crinan, Lord of Atholl and hereditary Abbot of Dunkeld, who married the daughter of Malcolm II (1005–34), and whose son was Duncan I (1034–40), the king supposedly murdered by MacBeth. In Gaelic the clan are refered to as *Clann Donnachaidh* ("Children of Duncan").

Another Duncan fought for Robert Bruce at Bannockburn; he was succeeded by Robert *Riabhach* ("Grizzled"), who captured the murderer of King James I, Sir Robert Graham, in 1437, and was rewarded by having his lands in Struan made a barony. It is this Robert who gave his name to the family, and the chiefly line have since been the Robertsons of Struan, or "Struan Robertsons".

The Robertsons were loyal supporters of the Stuarts. They fought in all Montrose's campaigns and played an important role in the Battle of Inverlochy (1645), and, after the Restoration, Charles II settled a pension upon Struan.

Alexander, "the poet-chief", was studying for the priesthood when he succeeded to the chiefship. He left his calling and joined Bonnie Dundee in 1688. Following King James' defeat, his estates were forfeited and he joined the

king in exile, returning under the general amnesty granted by Queen Anne (1703). In 1715 he again called out his clan when the Jacobite standard was raised, and again went into exile and returned under the general amnesty of 1725. He was pardoned in 1731, but joined Prince Charlie in 1745 with his clan. By this time he was too old to fight, so returned home in Sir John Cope's carriage after the Battle of Prestonpans.

The barony of Struan was restored to Alexander's descendant, also named Alexander, in 1784, and the chiefship eventually passed to a branch of the family which had settled in Jamaica.

Ross

Lands:	Ross-shire
Motto:	*Spem successus alit*
	("Success nourishes hope")
Plant Badge:	Juniper

The clan takes its name from the old county of Ross (in Gaelic *ros* means "promontory"), of which their chiefs were earls from about 1226. The first Earl, *Fearchar Mac in t'sacairt* ("the Son of the Priest", the priest being the hereditary Abbot of Applecross) brought an army out of the north to assist the recently crowned King Alexander II in 1215 against rival claimants. He "mightily overthrew the king's enemies", was knighted and later given the Earldom of Ross.

The first five chiefs were Earls of Ross, then the earldom passed to the daughter of the last chief, Euphemia, while the chiefship went to her half-brother, Hugh Ross of Balnagowan (1372). Euphemia's inheritance was repeatedly challenged, ultimately successfully by the Lord of the Isles, and when the Lordship was forfeited in 1476, the title passed to the Crown. David, 12th Chief, brought 1000 men to fight for Charles I at the Battle of Worcester (1651), and spent two years in the Tower of London as a result. On the death of his son, also named David, the chiefship passed to a remote branch, but was restored to the true line in 1903.

One of the descendants of Hugh Ross of Balnagowan was Colonel George Ross, a signatory of the American Declaration of Independence; another was Sir Ronald Ross of Sandwick, who discovered the cause of malaria and was awarded the Nobel Prize for Medicine in 1902.

Stewart

Lands:	Bute, Appin, Atholl
Slogan:	(different for each branch)
Plant Badge:	Thistle, Oak

The family name derives from its chiefs being hereditary Stewards of Dol in Brittany and later of Scotland, a position granted to their ancestor Walter Fitz Alan by King David I in 1124. Following the marriage of Robert Stewart to Marjory, daughter of Robert the Bruce, and the subsequent death of her brother, King David II, in 1371, the Stewarts provided the Royal House. The male line of this dynasty ended with the death of Cardinal Henry, Duke of York, brother of Prince Charles Edward Stewart, in 1807.

Many families descended from the Royal line. Stewarts hold or have held the Dukedoms of Albany, Rothesay and Lennox, the Marquessate of Bute and the Earldoms of Menteith, Buchan, Angus, Atholl, Strathearn, Carrick, Buchan and Galloway. Among the Highland branches of the family were the Stewarts of Bute, Appin, Ardvorlich and Atholl.

Stewart is sometimes written "Stuart". This began when Mary, Queen of Scots (1542–67) married the Dauphin when she was 16 and returned to Scotland two years later, both a Queen of France and a widow. Since the French have no "w" her surname was rendered as "Stuart", and the spellings have since been interchangeable. The Highland Stewarts tend to favour the original, "ew", spelling.

The Royal Stewart tartan is the personal tartan of H.M. The Queen and is wearable by all her subjects. At the last count there were 58 other Stewart tartans.